the SCHOOL HOUSE ROCK!™ songbook

Piano/Vocal Arrangements by Edwin McLean

 For a comprehensive listing of Cherry Lane Music's songbooks, sheet music, instructional materials, videos and more, check out our
entire catalog on the Internet. Our home page address is: http://www.cherrylane.com

Contents

The World Of

"I'm just a bill and I'm sittin' here on Capitol Hill. . .

"Well, I got this far. When I started I wasn't even a bill, I was just an idea. Some folks back home decided they wanted a law passed, so they called their local congressman, and he said, "You're right, there ought to be a law!" Then he sat down, wrote me out, and introduced me to Congress, and I became a bill, and I'll remain a bill until they make me a law."

"Conjunction Junction, what's your function? Hookin' up words and phrases and clauses. Conjunction Junction, how's that function? I got three fav'rite cars that get most of my job done. Conjunction Junction, what's their function? I got 'and,' 'but' and 'or'; they'll get you pretty far."

"She travels like a rocket with her comet team, and there's never been a planet Janet hasn't seen. No, there's never been a planet Janet hasn't seen. She's been to the sun; it's a lot of fun. It's a hot spot, it's a gas! Hydrogen and helium in a big, bright glowing mass! It's a star! It's a star. . ."

SCHOOLHOUSE ROCK

Once upon a time, way back in 1973, an advertising executive wondered why his son could remember every lyric of every Rolling Stones song, but couldn't memorize his times tables to save his life. He enlisted a creative team to come up with an educational phonograph record, and "Three Is A Magic Number" was born. The song was so lyrically vivid, so vibrant, that an entire animated musical short was developed—a music video, well before the advent of 24-hour music video channels. It landed a spot on ABC's Saturday morning programming, and *Schoolhouse Rock* was born.

Over a thirteen-year period, six series were developed: *Grammar Rock, Multiplication Rock, America Rock, Science Rock, Money Rock* and *Computer Rock*. The videos in each series meshed quirky cartoon characters, lively, unforgettable melodies and rhythms, and inimitable (and educational!) lyrics. "I'm Just A Bill," "Conjunction Junction," "My Hero, Zero" and all the rest demonstrated that education could be fun, and that knowledge truly is power.

Today a new generation of Saturday morning television viewers is hooked on the singular images, music and message of *Schoolhouse Rock*—in much the same way their parents were, and *still* are. What that translates into is that millions more of us instinctively know that the response to "Conjunction Junction" is "What's your function?," along with the series' other priceless lyrical quips and musical hooks.

I'm Just A Bill

Words and Music by
Dave Frishberg

Medium Rock

Boy: *Wheh! You sure gotta climb a lotta steps to get*

to this Capitol building here in Washington! Well, I wonder who that sad little scrap of paper is?

I'm just a bill,—— yes, I'm on-ly a bill,—— and I'm sit-tin' here on Cap-i-tol Hill.——
I'm just a bill,—— yes, I'm on-ly a bill,—— and I got as far as Cap-i-tol Hill.——
I'm just a bill,—— yes, I'm on-ly a bill,—— and if they vote for me on Cap-i-tal Hill,—

To Coda

and I'll remain a bill until they decide to make me a law.

Boy: *Listen to those congressmen arguing!* *Is all that discussion and debate about you?* Bill: *Yeah, I'm one of the lucky ones.*

Most bills never even get this far. *I hope they decide to report on me favorably,*

Lolly, Lolly, Lolly
(Get Your Adverbs Here)

Words and Music by
Bob Dorough

Recitation

Lolly, Sr.: *Hello, folks, this is Lolly, Sr., saying we have every adverb in the book, so come on down and look.*

Lolly, Jr.: *Hello, folks, Lolly, Jr. here. Suppose your house needs painting; how are you going to paint it? That's where the adverb comes in. We can also give you a special intensifier, so you can paint it very neatly, or rather sloppily.*

Little Lolly: *Hi! Suppose you're going nut gathering; your buddy wants to know "where" and "when." Use an adverb and tell him!*

Use it with an ad - jec - tive, it says much more;—
Use it with a verb, it tells us how you did;—

an - y - thing de - scribed can be de - scribed some more.—
where it hap - pened, where you're go - ing, where you've been.—

An - y - thing you'd ev - er need is in the store,— and so you choose ver - y care - ful - ly
Use it with an - oth - er ad - verb; that's the end— and e - ven

ev - 'ry word you use.   more.   How, where, or

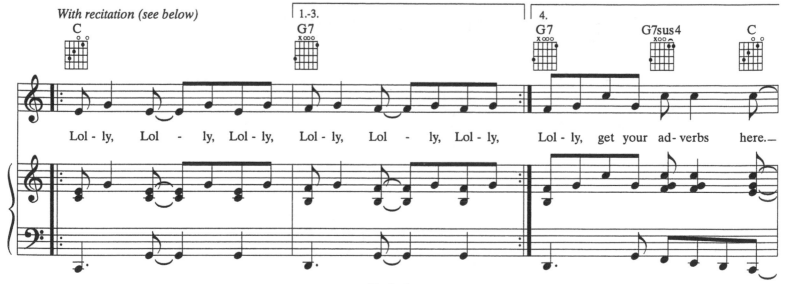

With recitation (see below)

Lol - ly, Lol - ly, Lol - ly, Lol - ly, Lol - ly, Lol - ly, Lol - ly, get your ad - verbs here.—

Recitation:

Announcer: *If it's an adverb, we have it at Lolly's.*
Bring along your old adjectives, too,
like "slow," "soft," and "sure."
We'll put 'em out with our "L-Y"
attachment and make perfectly
good adverbs out of them.

With recitation (see below)

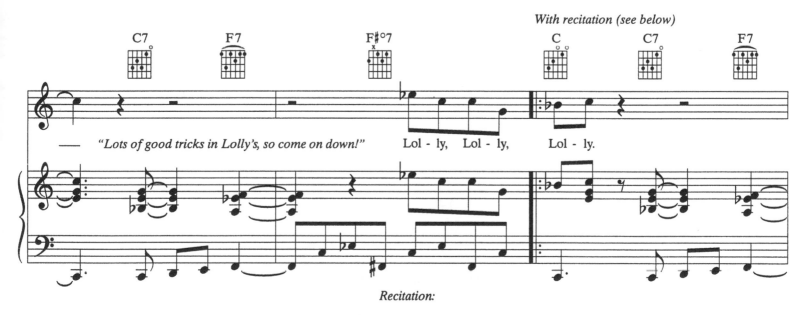

— *"Lots of good tricks in Lolly's, so come on down!"*   Lol - ly, Lol - ly, Lol - ly.

Recitation:

Announcer: *Adverbs deal with manner, place, time!*
Condition, reason! Comparison, contrast!
Enrich your language with adverbs!

Lolly, Jr.:   *Besides, they're absolutely free!*

Play 5 times

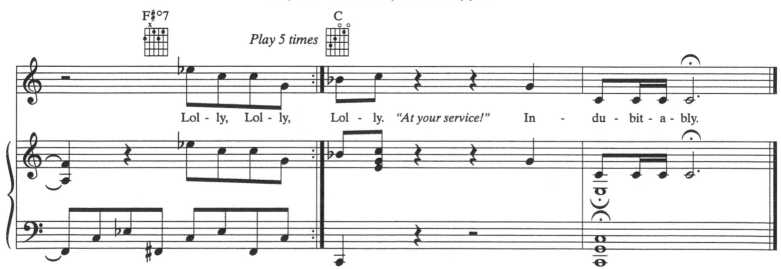

Lol - ly, Lol - ly, Lol - ly. *"At your service!"*   In - du - bit - a - bly.

17

Conjunction Junction

Words and Music by
Bob Dorough

Con - junc - tion Junc - tion, what's ____ your func - tion? Hook - in' up words and

phras - es and claus - es. Con - junc - tion Junc - tion, how's ____ that func - tion? ____ I got

three fa-v'rite cars ___ that get most ___ of my job ___ done. Con-junc-tion Junc-tion, what's ___

___ their func - tion? ___ I got "and," "but," and "or"; they'll get you pret-ty far. ___

"And"... that's an additive, like "this" and "that." "But"... that's sort of the opposite,

not this, but that. And then there's "or," "O - R." When you have a choice like this or that,

21

The Great American Melting Pot

Words and Music by
Lynn Ahrens

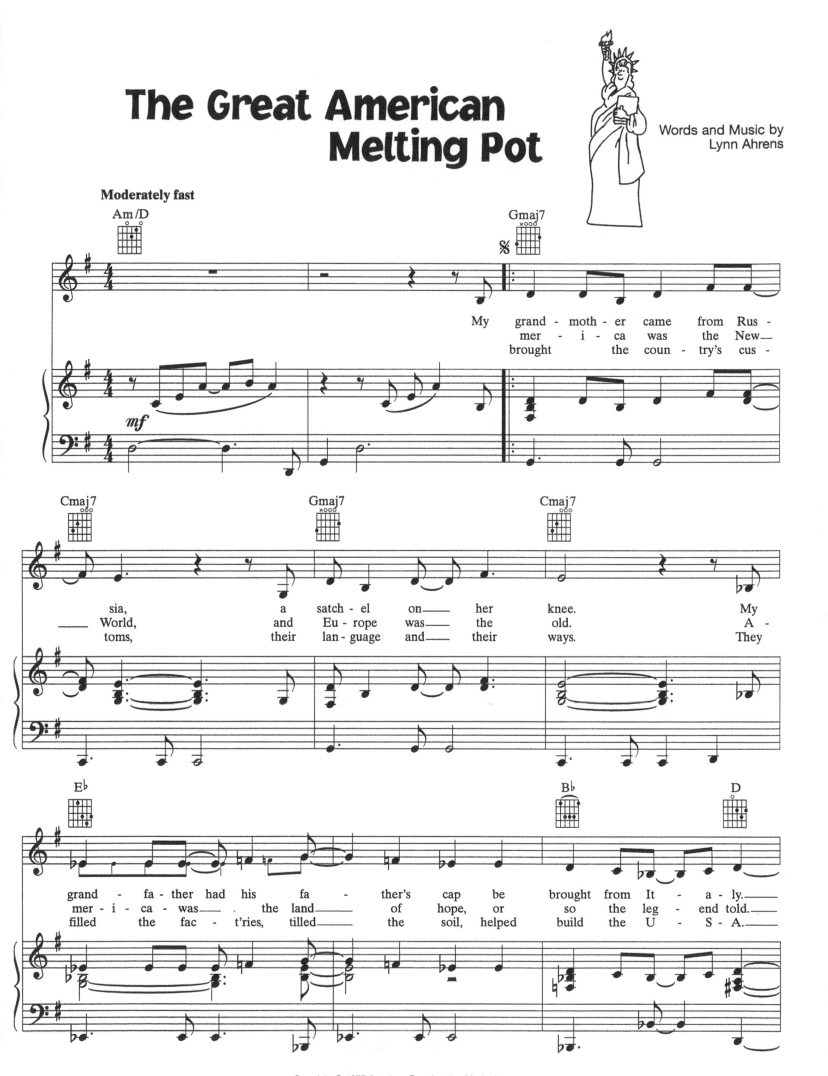

Moderately fast

My grand-moth-er came from Rus-sia, a satch-el on her knee. My
grand-fa-ther had his fa-ther's cap be brought from It-a-ly.

A-mer-i-ca was the New World, and Eu-rope was the old.
A-mer-i-ca was the land of hope, or so the leg-end told.

brought the coun-try's cus-toms, their lan-guage and their ways. They
filled the fac-t'ries, tilled the soil, helped build the U-S-A.

They'd_____ heard a - bout a coun - try where_____
On_____ steam - boats by the mil - lions, in_____
Go on and ask_____ your grand - ma, hear_____

life might let_____ them win; they paid the fare_____ to A -
search of hon - est pay, those nine - teenth cen - t'ry
what she has_____ to tell; how great to be_____ A -

mer - i - ca, and there they melt - ed in._____
im - mi - grants sailed to reach the U - S - A._____
mer - i - can and some - thing else_____ as well._____

Love - ly La - dy Lib - er - ty,___ with her book of rec - i - pes,___

and the fin - est one she's got___ is the great A - mer - i - can

melt - ing___ pot,___ the great A - mer - i - can melt - ing___ pot.___ A -

mer - i - ca was found - ed by the Eng - lish, but al - so by the Ger - mans, Dutch, and French. The

prin-ci-ple still sticks; our her-i-tage is mixed. So an-y kid could be the Pres-i-dent. You sim-ply

melt right in.___ It does-n't mat-ter what your skin.___

___ It does-n't mat-ter where you're from,___ or your re-li-gion. You

jump right in_____ to the great A-mer-i-can melt-ing___ pot,___

Interplanet Janet

Words and Music by
Lynn Ahrens

Bright and lively

They say our so-lar sys-tem is cen-tered 'round the sun; nine plan-ets, large and small, pa-rad-ing by. But some-where out in

space, there's an-oth-er shin-ing face that you might see___ some

night up in the sky.___

In-ter-plan-et Jan-et, she's a gal-ax-y girl,___ a so-lar sys-tem Miz from a

fu-ture world.___ She trav-els like a rock-et with her com-et team,___ and there's

So Jan-et got an au-to-graph!____

Mer-cu-ry was near the sun; so Jan-et stopped by, but the mer-cu-ry on Mer-cu-ry was much too high.____ So Jan-et split for Ve-nus, but on Ve-nus she found____ she could-n't see a thing for all the clouds a-round.____

Electricity, Electricity

Words and Music by
Bob Dorough

When you're in the dark,— and you want to see,— you need uh...

(Bkgd. vocal:) E - lec - tric - i - ty, e - lec - tric - i - ty.—

Flip that switch— and
Ev - 'ry build - ing

what do you get?— You get uh...
must be— wired— to use it uh...

E - lec - tric - i - ty, e - lec - tric - i - ty.

it comes;— they're bring-in' uh...
by an - y means;— you're mak-in' uh...

E - lec - tric - i - ty, e - lec - tric - i - ty.

A generator is a machine that contains a powerful magnet that creates a magnetic field.

When wires are rotated rapidly

through this field, then a current of electricity is produced.

Now, if we only had a superhero who could

stand here and turn the generator real fast,

then we wouldn't need to burn so much fuel

to make e -

E - lec - tric - i - ty,

e - lec - tric - i - ty.

E - lec - tric - i - ty, e -

40

Dollars And Sense

Words and Music by
Dave Frishberg

Becky Sue: You know, I love country music, and I
sounds pret-ty nif-ty, Mis-ter

prac-tice dai-ly on my out o' tune, cock-a-ma-mie u-ku-le-le; but my
Bank-er Dude;— you know I'd like to be thrift-y, but I ain't in the mood.— I'm in-

dai-ly u-ku-le-le play-in' ain't gon-na get me far.—
spired— and I'm writ-in' me a brand-new— coun-try song.—

I need a gui-tar, an amp, and some quad-ra-phon-ics, and
I got a lot o' coun-try west-ern in my blood, like

sev-'ral hun-dred dol-lars' worth of e-lec-tron-ics if I'm ev-er gon-na get to be a
Re-ba and Lo-ret-ta and Wi-no-na Judd; got-ta get me that e-quip-ment, and I

coun-try west-ern star!
ain't a-bout to wait too long!

*Becky Sue: Got-ta get me some

*2nd time: Both

dol-lars and sense, dol-lars and sense; them

45

out, young la - dy, no need to fret.— Al - though you can't af - ford to get that new e -

quip - ment yet,— you got a cou - ple hun - dred bucks saved up in your birth - day

stash. Why not de - pos - it them dol - lars in the

bank in - stead,— then at the end of the year you'll come out way a - head,— be - cause the

life is one ex - per - i - ence____ that spares us no ex -

pense, ____ got - ta use them dol - lars with a lit - tle bit of com - mon

sense. We got - ta use them dol - lars with a

lit tle bit of com - mon sense.

My Hero, Zero

Words and Music by
Bob Dorough

"Zero?"
"Yeah, Zero is a wonderful thing. In fact, Zero is my hero."
"How can Zero be a hero?"
"Well, there are all kinds of heroes, you know. A man can get to be a hero for a famous battle he fought, or by studying very hard and becoming a weightless astronaut. And then there are heroes of other sorts, like the heroes we know from watching sports. But a hero doesn't have to be a grown-up person, you know; a hero can be a very big dog who comes to your rescue, or a very little boy who's smart enough to know what to do. But let me tell you about my favorite hero..."

you could try.___ With ten bil - lion ze - roes,___

from the cave - men till the he - roes___ who in - vent - ed you, they

count - ed on their fin - gers and toes.___ *"And maybe some sticks and stones," "or rocks and bones," "their neighbors' toes."*

And no - bod - y real - ly knows___ how won - der - ful you

are._____ Why, we could nev - er reach the star with - out you, Ze - ro,___ my

he - ro,___ Ze - ro;___ how won - der - ful you are!

Place one ze - ro af - ter an - y num - ber, and you've mul - ti - plied that num - ber by ten.___

(See how eas - y that is?)___ Place two ze - roes af - ter an - y num - ber and you've

No More Kings

Words and Music by
Lynn Ahrens

Rather fast

Rock - in' and a - roll - in', splish - in' and a - splash - in', o - ver the ho - ri - zon, what

can it be?

The pil - grims sailed the sea ___ to find a
They plant - ed corn, you know; ___ they built their
He e - ven has the nerve ___ to

this point I don't care.
proud of us_ to - day._
tea in his - to - ry!_

Oh, they were
They knew that
They want - ed

miss - in' Moth - er Eng - land;_
now they'd run_ their own_ land;_
no more Moth - er Eng - land;_

they swore their loy - al - ty un - til the ver - y end._
but George the Third still vowed he'd rule them to_ the end._
they knew the time had come for them to take_ com - mand._

An - y - thing you say, King, it's o - kay,____ King; you know it's kind - a
An - y - thing I say, do it my way____ now. An - y - thing I
It's ver - y clear, you're be - ing un - fair,____ King, no mat - ter what you

scar - y on your own.____ Gon - na build a new land the way we____
say, do it my way.____ Don't you get to feel - ing in - de - pend -
say, we won't o - bey.____ Gon - na hold a rev - o - lu - tion now,____

To Coda

1.

— planned; would you help us run it till it's grown?____
ent,____ 'cause I'm gon - na force you to o - bey.____
— King,____ and we're gon - na

He taxed their prop-er-ty,___ he did-n't give them an-y choice.___ And back in Eng-land,___ he did-n't give them an-y voice.___ *That's called tax -*

a - tion with-out rep - re - sen - ta - tion, and it's not fair! But when the

col - o - nies com- plained, the King said: "I don't

care!"

D.S. al Coda

Coda

run it all our way. With no more kings, *(We're gonna elect a President!)*

Three Is A Magic Number

Words and Music by
Bob Dorough

Three is a mag-ic num-ber; yes, it is.___ It's a mag-ic num-ber.

Some-where___ in the an-cient, mys-tic trin-i-ty,___ you get three___

as a mag-ic num-ber. The

past and the pres-ent and the fu-ture, faith and hope— and char-i-ty, the

heart and the brain and the bod-y, give you three as a mag-ic

num-ber. It takes three legs to make— a tri-pod, or to

mf

one, twen - ty - four, twen - ty - sev - en, thir - ty.

Three, six, nine, twelve, fif - teen, eight - een,_____ twen - ty -

one, twen - ty - four, twen - ty - sev - en, thir - ty. *Multiply backwards from three times ten.*

Three times ten is thir - ty. Three times nine is twen - ty - sev - en.

Three times eight is twen-ty-four. Three times sev-en is twen-ty-one.

Three times six___ is eight-een. Three times five is fif-teen.

Three times four is twelve, and three___ times three is nine,___ and three times two is

six, and three times one is three, of course.___

one: What is—— it?   *Three!*   That's a mag - ic num - ber.

A man and a wom - an had—— a lit - tle ba - by.

Yes, they did.——   They had

three—— in the fam - i - ly.——   That's a mag - ic num - ber.——

rit.